The Perfect London Walk

S0-ADF-579

. . . a section of London where tourists are rarely seen. From the cottage where Keats wrote "Ode to a Nightingale" to Karl Marx's grave, the itinerary passes many fascinating and neglected spots. —Bloomsbury Review

There is admittedly no such thing as "the" perfect London walk, but this book may come close to providing a perfect day in London. Beginning with a stroll through the leafy streets of Hampstead, the reader visits Keats House and then climbs to the top of Parliament Hill for a panoramic view of London. Then there's a bracing walk across Hampstead Heath, to lunch at the Spaniards Inn. After a visit down the road to Kenwood House, with its Rembrandt self-portrait and its Adam library, the reader plunges into the Gothic gloom of Highgate Cemetery, where many eminent Victorians are still to be found.

Even visitors who are familiar with some of the places visited may be intrigued with the notion of combining them into a full day with fresh air, a walk on the Heath, lunch at the Spaniards, and teatime at Kenwood before a descent into the mysteries of London's most haunting cemetery.

The photographs provide a step-by-step walker's guide, and the text includes observations from those who have passed this way before, including Keats, Coleridge, Dickens, and Ian Nairn.

Even if you could get a taxi, Ebert and Curley's Perfect London Walk is worth taking. —MICHAEL CAINE

THE PERFECT LONDON WALK

by Roger Ebert and Daniel Curley

with photographs by Jack Lane

Andrews and McMeel

A Universal Press Syndicate Company

Kansas City

First Printing, March 1986
Fourth Printing, July 1995

Library of Congress Cataloging-in-Publication Data

Ebert, Roger.
    The perfect London walk.

    1. London (England)—Description—1981–   —Tours.
2. Walking—England—London—Guide-books.   I. Curley,
Daniel.   II. Title.
DA679.E23   1986   914.21'204858   86-1221
ISBN 0-8362-7929-8

Cameron Poulter Design

You will have a pleasant walk today. I shall see you pass. I shall follow you with my eyes over the Heath.

—Letter from John Keats to Fanny Brawne, 1820

Introduction
Roger Ebert

For twenty years my favorite pastime has been to walk
around London. I visit the great city as often as I can, and
I set out from my hotel in the morning armed with maps
and books and a journal to write in and a sketchbook to
draw in. I always take my old copy of *Nairn's London,* by
Ian Nairn, which is the most passionate and acerbic guide
ever written about London. Sometimes I have a plan in
mind. I will, perhaps, be following a familiar route, such
as the Walk of the Three Parks (overland from St. James to
Notting Hill), the Day of the Three Houses (Sir John Soane's
Museum, Dr. Johnson's House and Lord Leighton's House),
or Around Southwark and into the Unknown. On days
when an umbrella is called for, I begin at Sicilian Avenue in
the bookstore named Skoob, have a glass of fresh-squeezed
orange juice in a coffee bar named Onion, and walk across
Red Lion Square (surveyed by Bertrand Russell's fierce
bronze bust) and past the Ethical Society to Lamb's Conduit
Street and Bernard Stone's irreplaceable Turret Bookshop. I
am one of those people who would rather walk in the rain
than in the sunshine.

However, there is one walk that is more than just familiar. It is ritual. It is one I have taken every time I have
visited London. I have walked it in snow and sleet, in
rain and cold, in burning hot drought, and, most often,
on perfect spring or autumn days. I have walked it fifty
times with a hundred friends, and I am not half through
with it yet.

In its general outlines, my favorite walk is known to
many Londoners who love to prowl about their city, but it
is just far enough away from the beaten path that most
tourists, even sophisticated ones, will not have found it. I
call it Curley's Walk, and it begins about four inches above
the top edge of most tourist maps of central London. It's
above and a little to the left of that intriguing bit of green

called Primrose Hill, which is where the map companies think the tourist's London should end.

The walk has its name because Daniel Curley first led me across the Heath and into the gothic jungle of Old Highgate Cemetery. I met Curley on the first day of my freshman year at the University of Illinois, where he was a professor of English, and he has remained mentor and friend ever since. When I was passing through London in January 1966, on my way home after a year at the University of Cape Town, he was in London with his family, writing short stories, and he suggested one day that we go for a walk. Our first walk so impressed me that I have spent two decades proving to my satisfaction that there is no end to the mysteries and wonders of London.

The centerpiece of Curley's Walk is a bracing ramble on the Heath, including a climb to the top of Parliament Hill, the tallest place in London, and a visit to the tumulus where Queen Boadicea is said to be buried (if she is not instead, as some claim, beneath Track Five at Paddington). The approach includes a visit to the birthplace of Orwell's *Keep the Aspidistra Flying,* and the cottage where John Keats wrote, and wooed Fanny Brawne. The destination on the far side of the Heath is the Spaniards Inn, where Dickens tells us Mrs. Bardell was arrested on her lawyer's charge of failure to pay costs in her suit against Mr. Pickwick. The walk includes Kenwood House, with its Adam library, its Rembrandt self-portrait, and its gardens and sloping lawns.

All of these wonders are overtures to the most extraordinary Victorian memory in London, Highgate Cemetery. A good many visitors know about the "new" side of the cemetery, where Karl Marx is buried. But the old side, across the road, was closed for years because of vandalism, and was reopened only in 1984 as a result of the labors of

the Friends of Highgate Cemetery. Tours of the old cemetery are offered hourly every day of the year except
Christmas Day, and no matter how much you might enjoy
the earlier portions of Curley's Walk, do not tarry so long
that you cannot arrive at Highgate by 3 P.M. from October
through March, or 4 P.M. from April through September.

Some Words of Explanation
Daniel Curley

*A workman once informed the author that he had daily
crossed the Heath to his employment for many years, but
he believed that he had scarcely ever found his way across
it by precisely the same path.*

— CAROLINE A. WHITE, *Sweet Hampstead,* 1903

This book undertakes to lead you across the Heath from
one known point to another by one of these innumerable
ways, any one of which would provide natural beauty, long
perspectives, surprising views, and if you are particularly
lucky, the soft, misty landscapes Constable loved to paint.
If you manage to elude our carefully tested directions, you
will still be somewhere very fine and can appreciate the
wisdom of the motto of that splendid introduction to
Mexico, *The People's Guide:* "Wherever you go, there
you are."

There may be patches of mud to work around. There
may be wet grass to cross. So wear your best walking
shoes or your oldest sneakers. And never go anywhere in
England without an umbrella no matter how the sky looks
when you set out.

The walk is organized around two basic facts: The pubs
open at 11 A.M. (noon on Sundays) and the last tour of the
west side of Highgate Cemetery is at 4 P.M. (3 P.M. from
October through March). We recommend starting early
enough to be on the Heath before 11 A.M. From most points
in central London, this probably means being on a tube
train headed for Belsize Park by 9 or 9:30 A.M. That will
give you time to discover and explore Keats's cottage and
walk past the Freemasons before it has opened. (You can
start a little later on Sundays, because on that day Keats
House is open only between 2 and 5 P.M., long after we
have passed it, and you will only be looking in through the

gate, not stopping.) It is important to recognize that although pubs are included on this walk, it is not a pub crawl, so you must not try to better the record of John McHugh, who in 1968 abandoned the walk at the George, scarcely 150 yards uphill from the Belsize Park tube stop. The Freemasons is the last and greatest hazard, where the faint of heart are confronted by a choice between its garden and the actual entrance to the Heath. Once you are on the Heath, there is nothing to do but persevere until you reach the Spaniards, the scheduled lunch stop.

Remember, if you get lost on the Heath, ask directions of anyone walking a dog. Dog owners almost always know the way home at the very least.

Approaches to the Walk

The usual approach, and the one we recommend, is to take the tube:

By Underground, take the Northern Line to the Belsize Park stop. If you are starting from Central London, be absolutely certain to take a train on the Edgware Branch, or you are likely to end up in Highgate, at the end of the walk instead of the beginning. Look for the illuminated signs over the tracks.

By Bus: Bus Route 24 ends at South End Green, right where we call your attention to the pizza parlor that was once a bookstore where George Orwell worked. Pick up the walk at that point.

By British Rail: For the special confusion of visitors, British Rail operates a system quite distinct from the Underground network. This, however, is recommended only to the intrepid and the lucky. If you decide to try it, the stop is called Hampstead Heath and is just a few yards farther along the recommended line of march. When you come up to street level and are facing the main road, turn right toward Keats Grove (unless you want to backtrack to the Orwellian pizza parlor or perhaps buy a pastry at the bakery).

If by any chance you do not follow through to the end of the walk and find yourself returning to central London by tube from the Hampstead or Belsize Park stops (perhaps you will have walked in a circle or have got on a bus going in the wrong direction), be sure to take the Northern Line's Charing Cross route.

Hours to Keep in Mind

Keats House: Monday through Saturday, 10 A.M. to 1 P.M. and 2 to 6 P.M.; Sundays, 2 to 5 P.M.; Easter, spring, and late summer bank holidays, 2 to 5 P.M. Hours may change; check in advance. Closed Christmas, Boxing Day, New Year's Day, Good Friday, Easter Eve, and May Day. Admission free.

Kenwood: Open daily, 10 A.M. to 7 P.M., April through September; 10 A.M. to 5 P.M. October, February, and March; 10 A.M. to 4 P.M. November, December, and January. Closed Good Friday, Christmas Eve, and Christmas Day. Admission free.

Highgate Cemetery: The gates of the east side are locked closed at 4:30 P.M. Monday through Saturday, 5 P.M. Sunday Tours are conducted on the west side by the Friends of Highgate Cemetery every day of the year except Christmas Day. Tours start every hour on the hour from 10 A.M. to 3 P.M. from October through March; 10 A.M. to 4 P.M. from April 1 through September. Tips are not expected, but a donation toward the upkeep of the cemetery is requested. To be on the safe side try to arrive at the cemeteries no later than 3 P.M. And if you must choose, forgo the east side and Karl Marx's tomb to spend more time in the shady gloom of the extraordinary west part.

Pub opening hours: Monday through Saturday, 11 A.M. to 3 P.M., 5:30 to 11 P.M. Sunday, noon to 2 P.M., 7 to 10:30 P.M.

The Perfect London Walk

This map shows the area covered at a scale of approximately 4½ inches to the mile. Reproduced from the Ordnance Survey Map with the permission of the comptroller of Her Majesty's Stationery Office. Crown copyright reserved.

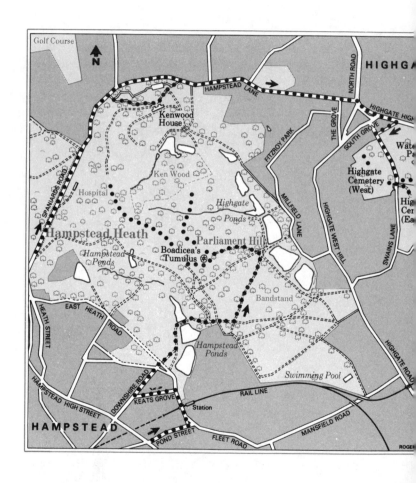

Take the Edgware Branch of the Northern Line to the Belsize Park tube stop, and exit onto Haverstock Hill.

Turn right and walk along the street.

Continue past the George Inn.

The George is a typical example of a London pub, delightfully deserted in the morning, delightfully crowded at night.

Perhaps a word about London pubs in general is in order. They are often divided into sections called Public Bar, Saloon Bar, or Private Bar. Anyone can go into any of these, but most people feel more comfortable in one than the other. The price of drinks varies slightly with the quality of the surroundings. The Public Bar is, as its name implies, the most democratic. Drinks are the cheapest there. Furnishings are barest. The company least pretentious.

Not all pubs are divided any longer; class distinctions seem to be made between one pub and another, rather than between the rooms of the same pub. A plague of renovation has opened up interior spaces. Light and airiness are now preferred to the claustrophobic room divisions of traditional pubs. As a matter of principle, the authors of this book are opposed to all pub modernization.

. . . at a tavern, there is a general freedom from anxiety. You are sure you are welcome; and the more noise you make, the more trouble you give, the more good things you call for, the welcomer you are. . . . No, sir, there is nothing which has yet been contrived by man, by which so much happiness is produced as by a good tavern.

—DR. JOHNSON

Cross the street and turn half-right down Hampstead Green.

Continue down the lane. On your left are the crumbling remains of St. Stephen's Church.

Purple brick, here, and three kinds of stone: a great hulk on a sloping site with a brooding and bulgy central tower made into a macabre Gothic dirge, moody and flashing with unexpected poetic juxtapositions: weathered sandstone columns, or a gristly roundel of sculpture, or cheesy voussoirs eaten away so that they are now inset to the bricks.

—IAN NAIRN, *Nairn's London*

To the right is Royal Free Hospital. Near the same site in the nineteenth century stood a smallpox hospital and an insane asylum.

The Royal Free leaves little room for anything else on the south side of Pond Street. But . . . St. Stephen's Church is still there at the top, a dirty red-brick giant designed by Teulon in 1870. Before the hospital took over the inner atmosphere, the church looked not unimpressive on its corner beside Hampstead Green . . . Railed off to the south of the church is a triangle of grass from which many dying elms were recently removed. One way and another this corner of Hampstead has not fared well.

—IAN NORRIE,
   Hampstead: London Hill Town (Wildwood, 1981)

The path leads down to the Roebuck, with its pink totem high up on the façade.

Cross the street, turn right, and continue down the hill.

Sir Julian Huxley, the biologist, brother of Aldous, grand-son of T. H., lived here at No. 31 until his death in 1975. Aldous lived nearby in Hampstead Hill Gardens in 1919.

In the 1960s this pizza parlor was a popular cafe where Hampstead chess players sat for hours at tables lined up along the windows.

In 1934 and 1935, George Orwell worked in a bookstore called Booklover's Corner on this site:

Our shop stood exactly on the frontier between Hampstead and Camden Town, and we were frequented by all types from baronets to bus-conductors. . . . Many of the people who came to us were of the kind who would be a nuisance anywhere but have special opportunities in a bookshop. . . . There are two well-known types of pest by whom every second-hand bookshop is haunted. One is the decayed person who comes every day, sometimes several times a day, and tries to sell you worthless books. The other is the person who orders large quantities of books for which he has not the smallest intention of paying.

        —GEORGE ORWELL,
                "Bookshop Memories," in *The Collected Essays, Journalism and Letters of George Orwell* (1968)

Orwell used the bookstore for the setting of his novel *Keep the Aspidistra Flying:*

Dull-eyed, he gazed at the wall of books. He hated the whole lot of them, old and new, highbrow and lowbrow, snooty and chirpy. The mere sight of them brought home to him his own sterility. For here was he, supposedly a "writer," and he couldn't even "write"! It wasn't merely a question of not getting published; it was that he produced nothing, or next to nothing. And all that tripe cluttering the shelves—well, at any rate it existed; it was an achievement of sorts. . . . But it was the snooty "cultured" kind of books that he hated the worst. Books of criticism and belles-lettres. The kind of thing that those moneyed young beasts from Cambridge write almost in their sleep—and that Gordon himself might have written if he had had a little more money.

Turn the corner in front of the Pizza Parlor and walk along South End Road, paying special attention to the Hampstead Tea Rooms at No. 9, which will sell you a pastry from the window. Then continue to walk along, noticing on your right the Hampstead Heath station of British Rail.

When you see the sign for Keats Grove, turn left.

Although the street is now named for Keats, it was known when Keats moved here as Albion Grove, and was in a semirural setting. Keats first visited Hampstead in 1816, when it was already a residence for a good many writers, and here he met Leigh Hunt, Charles Armitage Brown, and (one day, in a place on the Heath we will pass before long) Samuel Taylor Coleridge.

You will come upon Keats House on your left. The opening hours are 10 A.M. to 1 P.M. and 2 to 6 P.M. on weekdays, and 2 to 5 P.M. on Sundays.

On the right of the walk, next to the library, is a plum tree planted on the spot where Keats heard his famous nightingale sing. Near this place one morning in May 1819, he put his chair under a tree and listened to the bird that had built its nest there, and he wrote in two or three hours his immortal "Ode to a Nightingale." Here are two of the stanzas:

I.

My heart aches, and a drowsy numbness pains
    My sense, as though of hemlock I had drunk,
Or emptied some dull opiate to the drains
    One minute past, and Lethe-wards had sunk:
'Tis not through envy of thy happy lot,
    But being too happy in thine happiness,—
That thou, light-winged Dryad of the trees,
    In some melodious plot
Of beechen green, and shadows numberless,
    Singest of summer in full-throated ease.

VII.

Thou wast not born for death, immortal Bird!
    No hungry generations tread thee down;
The voice I hear this passing night was heard
    In ancient days by emperor and clown:
Perhaps the self-same song that found a path
    Through the sad heart of Ruth, when, sick for home,
She stood in tears amid the alien corn;
    The same that oft-times hath
Charm'd magic casements, opening on the foam
    Of perilous seas, in faery lands forlorn.

In Keats House all you want to know—and more—will be made available to you. But you may take particular pleasure in noticing the portrait of Keats by Joseph Severn, the friend who was with him when he died in Rome. It shows Keats seated just so in one chair, with his arm resting on the back of another chair. You will also observe that in the middle of the floor, right where you can sneak a touch, are identical chairs. You sneak a touch. No harm done. However, the truth of the matter is actually better than the fancy. The chairs are not the original chairs but were recreated on the inspiration of the portrait at the expense of an Indian gentleman, who must have been something of a poet in his own right. At least his imaginative gesture speaks almost as movingly of the original chairs as Keats's ode speaks of the original tree, blown down in a storm, where his nightingale sang.

Keats moved into this house in 1818, when he was twenty-three, sharing it with his friend, Charles Armitage Brown. In 1819, an adjoining house was let to the widowed Mrs. Brawne and her daughter, Fanny, with whom Keats quickly fell in love. Their engagement was ended by Keats's death in Rome in 1821.

He was ill much of the time he lived in this house, in a sickbed in his bedroom on the upper floor. (The bed is

small, but large enough for Keats, who stood only slightly over five feet.) Sometimes he was not only ill but in despair as well, because he felt his love for Fanny Brawne was not wholly reciprocated. At times during his illness he could not even bear to have her letters read to him, and asked that they be buried with him instead. In the autumn of 1818 he wrote these "Lines Supposed to Have Been Addressed to Fanny Brawne" in the margin of another manuscript. It is easy to imagine him on his sickbed as he wrote it.

> *This living hand, now warm and capable*
> *Of earnest grasping, would, if it were cold*
> *And in the icy silence of the tomb,*
> *So haunt thy days and chill thy dreaming nights*
> *That thou would wish thine own heart dry of blood*
> *So in my veins red life might stream again,*
> *And thou be conscience-calm'd—see here it is—*
> *I hold it towards you.*

Continue up Keats Grove to the top.

Dame Edith Sitwell lived in No. 20, and died there in 1964.

Turn right at St. John's, Downshire Hill.

[Downshire Hill is] the best bit of Georgian Hampstead. Inflected half way down by the delightful front of St. John, which strides out from the wedge-shaped corner site as though it had arrived fresh that morning from Naples. Built in 1818, and still a proprietary chapel: the sunny, uncomplicated charm has affected the stucco and yellow brick around and it manages to escape the bijou archness which bedevils so much of Hampstead. The special thing about Downshire Hill is that the Heath is beckoning at the end of it, grass and trees shaded in like a Gainsborough, curving uphill out of the view, promising release . . . .

—IAN NAIRN, *Nairn's London*

This is the last "proprietary chapel" in London, so called because it is owned by the congregation. If you wish, step inside and, for the best view, climb the staircase to the gallery.

Constable lived on Downshire Hill in Nos. 25 and 26 in 1826. Olive Schreiner, author of *The Story of an African Farm* and for a time the mistress of Havelock Ellis, lived at No. 30 in 1885, and the poet Edwin Muir, at No. 7 in the 1930s.

Pass the Freemasons.

Or, if it is already open, you might want to linger for a time in its bars or gardens. There has been a pub on this corner since 1819; the present building was rebuilt in 1934, and the builders are said to have found the River Fleet running beneath its basement on its way to Hampstead Ponds. Kingsley Amis once frequented this pub and extolled its toasted sandwiches, but now a much more substantial fare is served—although we recommend delaying lunch until the Spaniards. The Freemasons was known for years as the home of the last surviving court in England for the seventeenth-century game of pall-mall. When we last visited, the manager told us that plans were under consideration to reestablish the game.

Continuing past the Freemasons, cross the road and enter Hampstead Heath.

This is the best entry to the Heath, because you lose the houses straight away. No wonder it is well-loved and well-used: the romantic abrupt scenery, a bit like the hilly parts of Shropshire, provides maximum effect in the smallest areas. . . . There is Nature fitting you like a glove, never uncomfortable, just made for healthy walks and happy dogs.

—IAN NAIRN, *Nairn's London*

The Heath consists of about eight hundred acres of common ground, to which the local residents traditionally had access, including the right to pasture their sheep. In 1829, the lord of the Manor of Hampstead, Sir Thomas Maryon-Wilson, attempted to build on the Heath in order to enforce his claim of ownership. His fight went on for forty years, but was successfully defeated by a series of local groups, and in 1871 the Heath was sold by his successor and became permanently open to the public.

Although you can easily walk straight ahead on a path that will lead between the ponds, stray to your right and walk down to the bank of the first of the Hampstead Ponds, which is reserved for waterfowl.

Walk along keeping the pond to your right. Across the water are the backs of the houses of South Hill Park, many of them with studios overlooking the water.

Now follow along to the left as the path follows the ponds around and climb up the slight rise to find a causeway leading between the second and third ponds.

The ponds are spring-fed, were dammed as early as 1589, and by the early eighteenth century were being used to provide water for the city. They were, of course, the subject of Samuel Pickwick's historic paper, "Speculations on the Source of the Hampstead Ponds, with Some Observations on the Theory of Tittlebats," which Dickens assures us was read to the Pickwickians on May 12, 1827.

Cross the causeway between the second pond and the bathing pond.

There are so many warnings of hazards such as deep water, thin ice and wild life which mustn't be disturbed, that even if I thought this a temperate enough climate to bathe in, I wouldn't risk it. Another thing. Dead bodies are not infrequently found floating, or on the bottom; according to the police, corpses are not uncommon anywhere on the Heath. So far I am glad not to have encountered one, and the causeway is almost certain to be free of them.

—IAN NORRIE, *Hampstead: London Hill Town*

Presented with a choice of paths on the far side of the ponds, do not turn sharp left along the bank of the pond (toward the "No Cycling" sign), but instead walk ahead. You may most easily bear slightly right and pass along a shady passage that will eventually lead to a paved path that climbs Parliament Hill.

However, for a memorable walk down a leafy corridor, find after a few yards a path opening on the left and follow it between old wooden fenceposts until . . .

. . . you find an opening on the right, with a little fenced lane leading up to an extraordinary gnarled tree.

As you emerge from the lane, turn half-right and you will see the gradual rise to Parliament Hill. If it is a muddy day, take the paved path to the right and follow it up to the top of the hill. Otherwise, just plunge straight ahead.

The summit of Parliament Hill is the highest place in London, as high as the spire of St. Paul's Cathedral, which you may be able to see on a clear day. Although an engraved tablet provides a key to the London cityscape below you, much of it is lost on a hazy day.

There are several theories about how Parliament Hill got its name, but no definitive explanation. *The London Encyclopedia* suggests, "it was from here that the Gunpowder Plotters were to watch the destruction of Parliament in 1605. It was also called Traitor's Hill."

There is even a theory that part of it is man-made:

[In 1660] a windmill occupied the summit of what is now known as Parliament Hill, where . . . the trench formed by the removal of its foundation is still to be traced.

. . . there is a tradition of Saxon times still extant in this neighborhood. Was it not about the skirts of Highgate that Alfred encamped with his troops to protect the citizens of London, whilst they gathered in the harvest from the surrounding fields, from Hastings of the Ivory Horn, who lay with his Danish army beside the Lea, ready to pillage them of their summer fruits? And might not some great battle have been fought, and have resulted in the raising of this mound?

—CAROLINE A. WHITE, *Sweet Hampstead* (1903)

As you face around, Highgate Village is on the hills to your right.

You will inevitably find interesting people atop Parliament Hill and as you walk across the Heath. On windy days, kite fliers make use of the hill, sometimes employing complicated equipment including reels, harnesses, and protective gloves. Hobbyists make use of all corners of the Heath. There is even a pond given over to the sailing of elaborate remote-controlled model boats, although it lies to the right of our suggested line of march.

The sixth of Leigh Hunt's Hampstead Sonnets describes this view:

A steeple issuing from a leafy rise,
*   With farmy fields in front, and sloping green,*
*   Dear Hampstead, is thy southern face serene,*
Silently smiling on approaching eyes,
Within, thine ever-shifting looks surprise,
*   Streets, hills, and dells, trees overhead now seen*
*   Now down below, with smoking roofs between—*
A village, revelling in varieties.
Then northward what a range, with heath and pond,
*   Nature's own ground, woods that let mansions through*
And cottaged vales with pillowy fields beyond,
And clump of darkening pines, and prospects blue,
And that clear path through all, where daily meet
Cool cheeks, and brilliant eyes, and morn-elastic feet!

Now walk downhill toward a grove of oaks that is at about eleven o'clock if you have your back squarely turned against London and the Post Office Tower. In a generally northwest direction lies your luncheon destination, the Spaniards Inn.

This is the beginning of the walk across the Heath. Although we will make a good effort to guide you safely across to the other side by a direct route, be warned that the odds are excellent that you will get lost. This is one of the hazards and one of the joys of any walk on the Heath. In all weathers, however, there are walkers on the Heath who will cheerfully provide directions. Just ask, "Which way to the Spaniards Inn?" Our experience has been that no two walkers give corresponding answers to that question, but in one way or another you should succeed in arriving at the other end of the Heath, where you will find yourself (a) on Spaniards Road, and should turn right and walk along to the Inn; (b) at the edge of the grounds of Kenwood, which you should skirt, saving them for later and keeping Kenwood to your right until you find Spaniards Road, which you follow to the right, or (c) somewhere along Hampstead Road, in which case you have veered off to the north, and can follow the road back to the left until you pass the entrance to Kenwood and then find the Spaniards Inn a bit further along.

When you reach the grove of oaks, pass through it and cross a meadow to find a second line of trees. Try to find a tree with a curious knob on its trunk and a white post nearby. It will be beside a little ditch, which you should hop across.

Continue straight ahead, past these trees. Although many trees admittedly look alike, just continue in a straight line past these, and you will soon see a compact grove of trees ahead of you.

Within this grove is a tumulus, or prehistoric gravesite. Legend calls it the burial place of Queen Boadicea of the Iceni, a tribe well known to crossword puzzle fans. After the death of her husband, who tried to protect her by willing much of his wealth to the Emperor Nero, she was deposed and humiliated. But she bided her time, and raised a rebellion, leading her people from the east in a war that wiped out the Roman Ninth Legion, seventy thousand Romans, the cities of Colchester and Verulam, and parts of London. When the Romans finally defeated her in A.D. 61, she either killed herself with poison or died of rage (the stories vary).

The mound is regularly violated or honored by visits of Druid worshipers and black magicians, who offer sacrifices to the spirit of the dead queen, and leave behind the blood and bones of chickens. There are often dead ashes at the summit. Perhaps to discourage Druidical rites, there is usually a padlock on the gate to the iron fence. Additional discouragement is the London folk legend that the queen is actually buried under Track No. 5 at Paddington Station.

Just beyond the tumulus, find a hard path and follow it toward the left. After a while it is no longer paved.

Continue to follow it beneath some trees.

Notice on the left an avenue of trees. This was one of Keats's favorite spots, and it was probably here that he met Coleridge for the first time. Many years later Coleridge recalled the meeting:

A loose, slack, not well-dressed youth met Mr. Green and myself in a lane near Highgate. Mr. Green knew him and spoke. It was Keats! He was introduced to me and stayed a minute or so. After he had left us a little way, he came back and said, "Let me carry away the memory Coleridge of having pressed your hand!"

"There is death in that hand," I said to Green, when Keats was gone; yet this was, I believe, before consumption shewed itself distinctly.

—August 14, 1832, *Table Talk of S. T. Coleridge*

This was not the only time Coleridge made a similar prediction, and he was eventually always proved right.

Keats remembered their historic meeting somewhat differently:

Last Sunday I took a Walk towards Highgate and in the lane that winds by the side of Lord Mansfield's park I met Mr. Green our Demonstrator at Guy's in conversation with Coleridge . . .

I walked with him at his alderman-after-dinner pace for near two miles I suppose. In those two Miles he broached a thousand things—let me see if I can give you a list—Nightingales, Poetry—on Poetical Sensation—Metaphysics—Different genera and species of Dreams—Nightmare—a dream accompanied by a sense of touch—single and double touch—A dream related—First and second consciousness—the difference explained between will and Volition—so say metaphysicians from a want of smoking the second consciousness—Monsters—the Kraken—Mermaids—Southey believes in them—Southey's belief too much diluted—A Ghost story—Good morning—I heard his voice as he came towards me—I heard it as he moved away—I had heard it all the interval—if it may be called so. He was civil enough to ask me to call on him at Highgate. Good night!

—Letter from Keats
to his brother, April 1819.

Press forward into a grove of trees.

If you see this gate on the right, do not enter it. It leads to the grounds of Kenwood House, which we will approach from another route. You may see a distant view of Kenwood, but bear slightly left and ahead.

Plunge into the dark woods at the left, more or less straight ahead.

A solitary birch marks the way. Continue ahead keeping an iron fence on your right.

You will emerge to find a narrow path beside a grassy field. At the far end of this field there is a bench, where you might want to pause for a time.

Keats is supposed to have written "I Stood Tiptoe Upon a Little Hill" as a result of resting on a beautiful summer day in a field near Kenwood, perhaps the same field we now regard. We quote only the opening passage.

I stood tiptoe upon a little hill,
The air was cooling, and so very still
That the sweet buds which with a modest pride
Pull droopingly, in slanting curve aside,
Their scantly-leaved, and finely tapering stems,
Had not yet lost those starry diadems
Caught from the early sobbing of the morn.
The clouds were pure and white as flocks new shorn,
And fresh from the clear brook; sweetly they slept
On the blue fields of heaven, and then there crept
A little noiseless noise among the leaves,
Born of the very sigh that silence heaves:
For not the faintest motion could be seen
Of all the shades that slanted o'er the green.
There was wide wandering for the greediest eye
To peer about upon variety;
Far round the horizon's crystal air to skim,
And trace the dwindled edgings of its brim;
To picture out the quaint and curious bending
Of a fresh woodland alley, never ending;
Or by the bowery clefts, and leafy shelves,
Guess where the jaunty streams refresh themselves.
I gazed awhile, and felt as light and free
As though the fanning wings of Mercury
Had played upon my heels: I was light-hearted,
And many pleasures to my vision started;
So I straightway began to pluck a posey
Of luxuries bright, milky, soft and rosy.

As you leave the field behind, follow the path to the roadway you will soon be able to hear, and then to see, ahead.

Near here at the top of the Heath, but off to the left down this road and not on our line of march, is another famous pub named Jack Straw's Castle. Jack Straw was a leader of the Peasants' Revolt of 1381. The plague and an influx of Flemish weavers created hard times for the peasants, who marched on London and made their camp up at the top of the Heath. Richard II at this time of crisis performed the one memorable act of his reign (except, of course, for those Shakespeare invented for him). The king was only fifteen years old, but he rode out to confront the rebels single-handed. "I am your king," he said. "You shall have no leader but me." He placed himself at their head and marched them around the walls of London and sent them home with promises of redress of all their wrongs. Naturally, once they were all dispersed and safely at home, he sent around his officers, arrested the leaders of the revolt, and hanged them.

At this time Chaucer was a customs officer and not yet of any great prominence. He later made an allusion to these events in the "Nun's Priest's Tale." When the fox carries off the rooster Chanticleer, there is a terrible uproar:

> *So hideous was the noise, I'm telling you,*
> *Certainly Jack Straw and all his crew*
> *Never made shouts half so shrill*
> *When they would any Fleming kill*
> *As that same day were made upon the fox.*

The castle in the name of Jack Straw's Castle seems to come from the memory of prehistoric earthworks near the site.

When you come up to the Spaniards Road, turn right and follow the roadway until you come to the Spaniards Inn.

The Spaniards provides us with our luncheon destination.
In years past, the fare was limited to sandwiches and
"bangers," those greasy sausages that are so good with hot
English mustard. Now a buffet service has been installed in
a side room where once the pub dog slept uneasily in front
of a fireplace.

The Spaniards takes its name from a Spaniard, but which Spaniard is much in doubt. Some say a servant in the employ of the Spanish ambassador opened a tavern there on the Heath. Some say there were two Spaniards, brothers, who were the proprietors until one killed the other in a duel. And some say the Spanish ambassador to James I took refuge in the neighborhood during a time of plague. There has been a tavern on the spot since the seventeenth century at least, and the spot itself is an interesting one. The inn and the old toll house on the other side of the road create a bottleneck where the old toll booth must have been. This was most convenient for Dick Turpin, the celebrated highwayman. The room pointed out as Dick Turpin's Room looks directly onto the bottleneck, and it is easy to imagine Turpin at his ease, sizing up the travelers as they maneuvered past and deciding which ones were worth robbing.

Hampstead pubs are usually not much fun: they are like a private society whose performance is not worth the entrance fee—the intellectual equivalent of the Soho striptease club. But The Spaniards, at the very top of the Heath, gets a solid butt from its cockney visitors, at least in fine weather. The mixture shakes down very well; the warren of dark rooms, the big gardens, and this mingling of ages and classes make it more like a German beergarden than anywhere else I know in London. The atmosphere has all grown together, just like the slap-happy brick and weatherboard walls of the pub.

—IAN NAIRN, *Nairn's London*

Turpin's most notable feat was perhaps his celebrated ride from London to York in the course of a single night. He rode his mare, Black Bess, to death, while his pursuers used up twenty horses. Of course there are curmudgeons who maintain that no such ride ever did or ever could take place. Others observe that the ride to York had been a legend three hundred years before Turpin, and had been attached to the story of many popular heroes over the years, as is the case with any tale too good to let die.

Dickens was fond of stopping at the Spaniards, and he used the pub's garden as a setting for the unhappy day in *The Pickwick Papers* when Mrs. Bardell was arrested by the agents of Dodson and Fogg for nonpayment of legal costs in her suit against Pickwick. The arrest was preceded by a bittersweet tea party:

. . . in a couple of hours they all arrived safely in the Spaniards Tea-gardens, where the luckless Mr. Raddle's very first act nearly occasioned his good lady a relapse; it being neither more nor less than to order tea for seven; whereas (as the ladies one and all remarked), what could have been easier than for Tommy to have drunk out of anybody's cup—or everybody's, if that was all—when the waiter wasn't looking, which would have saved one head of tea, and the tea just as good!

. . .

"How sweet the country is, to be sure!" sighed Mrs. Rogers; "I almost wish I lived in it always."

"Oh, you wouldn't like that, ma'am," replied Mrs. Bardell . . .

"Oh! I should think you was a deal too lively and sought after to be content with the country, ma'am," said little Mrs. Cluppins.

"Perhaps I am, ma'am. Perhaps I am," sighed the first-floor lodger.

"For lone people as have got nobody to care for them, or take care of them, or as have been hurt in their mind, or that kind of thing," observed Mr. Raddle, plucking up a little cheerfulness, and looking round, "the country is all very well. The country for a wounded spirit, they say."

—CHARLES DICKENS, *The Pickwick Papers*

Leaving the garden of the Spaniards, turn left and walk along Hampstead Lane, until you see on the right the gatehouse for Kenwood.

There are many approaches to the house, some of them direct, some of them winding through beautifully landscaped grounds, which serve as a reminder that the two arts which the British gave to the world are watercolor painting and landscape gardening.

The trees in the park at Kenwood are said to be the splendid remnants of the great Middlesex Forest that once stretched from beyond the northern boundaries of the county almost to the walls of the city.

If you have followed paths around to the west lawns of Kenwood, you may sooner or later come across a curious thatched hut up a short flight of stairs. This is Dr. Johnson's Summer House, moved here from the Thrales' estate at Streatham, where Johnson often visited and where Mrs. Thrale, his friend and supporter, had the hut constructed so that he could meditate and write, shielded from summer heat and showers.

The summer house did not come to Kenwood easily. It was first moved to Ashgrove, in Kent, then back to Streatham Common, and finally to Kenwood. Its present location might well have pleased Johnson, for it looks over the garden and a sweep of lawn to the artificial pond and an even more artificial bridge, which looks as if you could walk over it, but is in fact only a prop. One would like to hear Johnson's comments on the bridge.

Johnson, the most formidable intellectual of his age, was nevertheless possessed of a simplicity and sweetness, as suggested by an entry in his memorandum book as he was sitting in his summer house at 3 P.M. August 9, 1781:

After innumerable resolutions formed and neglected, I have retired hither, to plan a life of greater diligence, in hope that I may yet be useful, and be daily better prepared to appear before my Creator and my Judge, from whose infinite mercy I humbly call for assistance and support.

The present house at Kenwood was built in the early eighteenth century, although there was a house on the site for at least a hundred years before that. In 1754 Lord Mansfield, the chief justice, took possession of the estate and ten years later engaged Robert Adam to remodel the house. During the Gordon Riots of 1780, Lord Mansfield's house in Bloomsbury was burned by a mob because it was popularly thought that he failed to entertain proper anti-Catholic sentiments and even went so far as to grant Catholics the full protection of the law.

After burning his town house (and his renowned library), the mob marched on Kenwood but fortunately stopped at the Spaniards to fortify themselves for the rest of their night's work. The landlord of the Spaniards kept the drink flowing and warned the Kenwood steward, who provided another barrel of ale and sent off for the cavalry. So Kenwood was saved by ale on that occasion, as it was later saved by Guinness stout, for the house was bought in 1925 by Lord Iveagh (Edward Cecil Guinness), and two years later under the terms of his will, it became public property together with the eighteenth-century pictures he had collected to complement the house.

The most famous painting in Kenwood is a magnificent late self-portrait by Rembrandt.

The collection (the Iveagh Bequest) is a long way removed from a country-house job lot. There is one of Rembrandt's most grandiose and level-headed self-portraits, and a Romney (Lady Albemarle) which balances exactly on the knife-edge of tender sympathy without sentimentality. Above all, there are two drumroll full length Gainsboroughs, in the Orangery. One (Lady Briscoe) is in his party-piece style: imperious figure, glistening grey dress, wonderful landscape behind in dashed-off diagonal brushstrokes. In the other (Countess Howe) figure and background are treated with equal sympathy and the result is a wonderful to-and-fro like the relation between house and park in a Repton landscape garden. Diaphanous wrap matches diaphanous trees, the honest face matches the honest clouds. A wonderful performance, as completely English as the Heath.

—IAN NAIRN, *Nairn's London*

The interior of Kenwood includes a library by Adam, which you will be permitted to peek into but not to enter. In the Orangery, pause long enough to absorb the remarkable fusion of the stately interior and the sweeping view.

Perhaps the view will lure you outside, on a warm day, to sit on the grass or on one of the benches given in memory of others who have enjoyed Kenwood. There is a restaurant in the old coach house, serving light lunches and teas.

Leaving Kenwood, return to Hampstead Lane and cross the road to catch the No. 210 bus into Highgate Village.

Alight in Highgate at the Rose and Crown.

The nearby Centaur Gallery is a series of surprises, unfolding like a Chinese box. From the window, a visitor guesses that the inside will be a single small, cluttered room. But the gallery unfolds down the hill in a series of rooms, leading to a sculpture garden and finally to converted stables containing modern art.

Cross the street on the zebra lines.

Find a narrow passage with a sign reading "To the Congregational Church." Pass through into a square.

If it is not much later than 2:30 P.M. (unlikely), you might want to make an optional detour at this point. Nearby, slightly off our line of march, are St. Michael's Church, where Coleridge is buried beneath the center aisle, and the Grove, a terrace of late seventeenth- and early eighteenth-century houses, where Coleridge lived at No. 3, the Gillman house, from 1823 until his death in 1834. He had come to Highgate in 1816 to live with Dr. Gillman in the hope that he could be cured of his addiction to opium.

The Poet was at first located on the second floor, next to the room occupied by my grandparents, but going up to reconnoitre one day the floor above, he was so delighted with the well-known view over Caen Wood and the adjacent valley that he requested his hosts to let his books and belongings be moved to this quaint upper chamber. His books on fixed shelves covered nearly one side of it from floor to ceiling.

—LUCY E. WATSON
   (granddaughter of his hosts), *Coleridge at Highgate*

Also nearby at 77 Highgate West Hill is the Flask, a splendid pub built in 1663 and rebuilt in 1767, featuring an inviting series of cozy rooms. It is unlikely that you will have arrived at this point before afternoon closing time, but if you have, there is no more convenient place to stop before braving the tombs of Highgate Cemetery.

So far Mason's map-reading had been flawless. He had come over Hampstead Heath, past Boadicea's tomb (legendary), past Jack Straw's Castle (reputed), past The Spaniards (notable for associations with Dick Turpin, if you like highwaymen, and with Mrs. Bardell, if you like Dickens—he himself liked both), through the grounds of Kenwood, stately-home-become-museum, and now he sat on a bench in the yard of The Flask, finishing a pint and poised for his final descent to the cemetery and the grave of Karl Marx.

—DANIEL CURLEY, "In the Hands of Our Enemies"

Cross the square and find the top of Swain's Lane, next to the minimarket. Walk down the lane toward Highgate Cemetery—and do not despair, we will not require you to climb back up this steep hill.

Keep your wits about you as you go down Swain's Lane. One of England's most brilliant scientists perished here by his own folly. On a cold winter day while riding in his carriage, Sir Francis Bacon conceived the notion that refrigeration might retard spoilage. No doubt he was cold himself and perhaps reflected that if he were to drop dead, he would be too cold to rot. The nearby cemetery walls encourage such thinking.

Unable to wait for proper laboratory conditions, Bacon stopped his carriage, got out, bought a chicken from a poor woman and stuffed it with snow. The woman was probably no genius but could have told him offhand that meat keeps better in winter than in summer. The results of Sir Francis's experiment were mixed: the chicken was pre-served, but Sir Francis was not. He caught a chill and was unable to reach his home in the Temple, so he begged asylum at the nearby house of his friend the Earl of Arun-del, perhaps best known as the collector of the Arundel Marbles. Unfortunately, although Sir Francis was warmly received at Arundel House, he was put into a cold bed, caught pneumonia, and died in the arms of his nephew, who bore the odd name of Sir Julius Caesar. It speaks well of the great man's character—although he did take bribes—that just before his death he dictated a letter to Arundel, praising the housekeeper for her care and diligence and magnanimously avoiding all mention of the cold bed.

After a time you will pass, on the left, the entrance to Waterlow Park (mark it for later). And then immediately there are the twin entrances to the two sides of Highgate Cemetery, the newer side on the left behind tall gates.

Check on the spot to ascertain when the Friends of Highgate Cemetery are conducting the next tour of the west cemetery. Our advice, if you must choose between the two sides, is to see the older west side. But we will save it for last, and begin by describing the east cemetery.

Enter through the gates and walk straight along until the path forks. Then bear left, until in two or three minutes' time you see the massive bust of Karl Marx. Flowers are invariably on the grave, left by delegations from people's republics.

Almost directly across from **Marx** is Herbert Spencer, philosopher and theorist. At one time in her life, George Eliot conceived a great passion for Spencer, and offered to accept any conditions just to be near him. He declined, but in death he did not escape her. See the next entry.

Turn back the way you came and retrace your steps to the first path on your right. Turn uphill and pass the first intersecting path and find the pillar of "George Eliot" (Mary Ann Cross) on your right.

Behind her grave and to the left (the corners just touch) is the grave of George Henry Lewes, her admirer, supporter, and lover. Her grave is well cared for—there are often fresh flowers—and his is buried in weeds.

John Walter Cross, whom George Eliot married shortly before her death, was twenty years younger than she and lived forty-four years after her death—until 1924 in fact. His grave is nearby, but it is even more obscure than that of Lewes, for we have never found it despite the fact that it is clearly marked on the cemetery's map.

If you visit George Eliot's grave in Highgate Cemetery,
you find it a model of decorum in a jungle
of unprincipled vegetation. Flowers miraculously
change their identity as the seasons change.
What were once pansies are now marigolds
and then back to pansies again in the spring.

If you know what you are looking for,
you can clamber over George Eliot's grave
(best not attempted in wet weather
for the marble is very slick)
and kick your way through ferns (bracken, Brit)
to the back left hand corner of the plot
(north east corner—that is if London runs true
north and south from the City to Highgate).
There you must part the ferns and find
(the schoolteacher who sets out the flowers
admits there is a limit to one woman's strength)
the grave of George Henry Lewes,
tactfully corner to corner,
the last secret touch
easing a secret pain.

—DANIEL CURLEY, "It's a Woman's World, George Eliot"

Retrace your steps out of the eastern cemetery, cross Swain's Lane, and enter the western side.

In the guard house by the gate, you are likely to find a few members of the Friends of Highgate Cemetery, who have rescued this remarkable place from neglect and obscurity.

After the bankruptcy in the 1970s of the United Cemeteries Company, which could trace itself back to the founding of the cemetery in 1839, the western side fell victim to decay, vandalism, and the depredations of satanic cultists. There was sporadic income from the use of the site as a location for Hammer horror films; look for Christopher Lee and Peter Cushing on the late show, creeping among the gravestones. But finally the gates were locked and the cemetery was closed to the public in 1975. Behind the walls, vegetation ran rampant and a considerable population of small wild animals flourished. Responding to this situation, the Friends of Highgate Cemetery was formed, took over ownership of the grounds, and began a program of preservation and conservation.

Members of the FOHC provide guided tours of the cemetery daily. The tour is free, but a voluntary contribution is asked to help with the upkeep of this extraordinary place.

The western cemetery is open only by guided tour, and the FOHC guides will point out many of the interesting graves. However, there is a map of the cemetery available with graves clearly indicated, and this may lead you to ask to be shown some grave of particular interest.

The honor of the "most requested" grave, a Friend of Highgate Cemetery once told us, is the one belonging to Elizabeth Eleanor Siddal, the model and wife of the pre-Raphaelite poet and painter Dante Gabriel Rossetti, buried in Highgate with Rossetti's family. Rossetti buried the manuscripts of some of his poems with her in 1862, only to decide in 1869 to reopen the grave and retrieve them.

IHS

IN THE
DEAR MEMORY OF
MY HUSBAND
GABRIELE ROSSETTI,
BORN AT VASTO AMMONE
IN THE KINGDOM OF NAPLES,
28TH FEBRUARY 1783,
DIED IN LONDON 26TH APRIL 1854.

JEREMIAH XXII. 10.
...TER COUNTRY, THAT IS AN HEAVEN
HEBREW XI. 10.
...AMI TU.
ALSO OF
FRANCES MARY LAVINIA,
BELOVED WIFE OF THE ABOVE NAMED
GABRIELE ROSSETTI,
BORN APRIL 27TH 1800, DIED APRIL 8TH 1886.

OF
WILLIAM MICHAEL ROSSETTI,
SON OF THE ABOVE,
BORN 25 SEPTEMBER 1829,
DIED 13 FEBRUARY 1919.
HAVING SEEN THE REALISATION OF ITALIAN ...

An anthology of horror . . .

This is the creepiest place in London; no Dickensian stretch of the river can match this calculated exercise in stucco horror, now itself decomposing. The entrance is well downhill in Swains Lane, and at first the landscape is ordinary. But as you wind up the hill it becomes more and more overgrown, choked in winter by dead fronds with an unnerving resemblance to spanish moss. The landscape looks less and less like London, more and more like Louisiana. Then, with a shock like a blood-curdling scream, the Egyptian entrance shows up. Beyond it, the Catacombs, a sunken rotunda lined with stucco-faced vaults, gently deliquescent, crumbling away. Inside them, coffins on ledges. A familiar name like Carl Rosa on one of the vaults seems to accentuate the terror. Nothing seems real but death at its greyest and clammiest. The cemetery closes well before dark, and a good job too.

—IAN NAIRN, *Nairn's London*

One of the famous occupants of the catacombs, inside the Egyptian entrance at the top of the cemetery, is Radclyffe Hall, author of the once-notorious *The Well of Loneliness,* a novel of lesbian love.

When we first came across this tomb, back in the days when it was still possible to wander freely in old Highgate, it was a sparkling oasis in the midst of a jungle. There was a polished steel gate through which we could see an altar with clean altar cloth, fresh flowers, and a lighted candle. We are not inventing this; we must have arrived just after a visit from one of her disciples. The black and white tile floor shone with a recent washing.

Now the gate is gone. The entrance is cemented over. On a recent visit, an FOHC guide assured us that a suit of Hall's male attire hangs on a rack inside the tomb. We doubt this.

It was a large iron gate, somewhat rusty, and gave the impression of not having been opened in a long time. The drive behind the gate was so broken and neglected that it showed only in patches the remains of a macadam surface. Trees and bushes crowded in from both sides and left only a glimpse along the gently curving avenue of tombs. Tall grass overwhelmed the smaller stones, and the whole place was so utterly ruinous that he felt an urge to visit it, to savor its melancholy and, perhaps, who knows, find the images of the tombs translating themselves into words and beginning the dance that would sooner or later crystalize into a poem. In the long run he had more faith in broken macadam than in Karl Marx.

—DANIEL CURLEY, "In the Hands of Our Enemies"

He saw, even before he took a step, that the broken macadam gave way to grass just a few yards up the hill, and as he committed himself to the drive, walls sprang up on either side. There was no gradual introduction. All at once the rows of monuments began, marble foundering in grass and trees, no space left that was not marble foiled in greenery, foiled in darkness. At first paths led off into the vacant jungle but even these soon disappeared, and there was no exit anywhere except here and there the hint of trodden grass scrambling between two stones and disappearing with a twist behind one of them. It was all darkness, but he could only try. Cautiously he left the drive and climbed the bank and passed behind a stone. Darkness and jungle. Gradually he made out the shapes of marble beneath the grass, within the bush, behind the vine. Gradually the marble city took shape in his mind, a Chichen Itza, an Angkor Vat of the imagination, although the one date which stood clear before him was barely fifty years old. Less than his own age. The dead branch he was staring at turned into an iron rose.

—DANIEL CURLEY, "In the Hands of Our Enemies"

After leaving Highgate Cemetery, walk a few yards uphill to the entrance of Waterlow Park. By strolling through the park in a generally uphill north by northeast direction, you will be able to avoid the torturous climb back up to the top of Swain's Lane.

Waterlow Park is named for Sir Sydney Waterlow, once Lord Mayor of London, who opened it in 1889 "to be a garden for those who are gardenless." The grounds were once the park of Lauderdale House, where Lady Arabella Stuart stayed in 1611 while en route to Durham, imprisonment, and death. Pepys and Marvell certainly visited at Lauderdale House, and lengend has it that Nell Gwynne did, as well.

Pass along the park's serene paths and ponds, to clear your mind of the cemetery's Gothic jungle. And, if you are lucky, there might be a concert in the band shell.

**You will probably emerge from Waterlow Park some-
where along Dartmouth Park Street. Go uphill to the
church on the corner, and you will reach the corner
of Highgate Hill Street.**

At this point, you must choose between returning home
via bus or the Archway tube, cr continuing the day by
going for tea in Highgate. If you turn left and climb Highgate High Street, you will find several places to have tea,
and you may even want to stop in at the Fisher & Sperr
bookshop, where there are not only countless books but
also inexpensive nineteenth-century engravings of some of
the places we have passed in Highgate and on the Heath.
Like the Centaur Gallery, the bookshop's size is deceptive;
zoning regulations forbid building above the street's roof-
line, and so the shop extends downhill in the rear, shel-
tering many more books than you might think.

If, on the other hand, you are still standing in front of the church at the corner of Dartmouth Park street, and would rather return home for your tea, the Archway tube station is down Highgate Hill, a relatively short but often welcome bus ride at this point.

If you elect to ride, cross the street to the bus stop a little way up the hill. For Hampstead, do not cross the road but go uphill to the bus stop. In both cases, the bus is the No. 210. For Archway, get off at Archway. For Hampstead, get off at Jack Straw's Castle and walk down to Hampstead Village.

If you decide to walk down Highgate Hill to the Archway tube and take the Northern Line back home, the bonus is the discovery of the stone marking the spot where Dick Whittington sat down and heard Bow Bells. The stone, surmounted by a handsome bronze of his cat, was for many years outside the decrepit old Whittington and Cat pub, but has now been moved down the hill to in front of the Whittington Stone pub.

According to legend, Whittington was a poor boy, a scullion in the house of a great merchant. It was the custom in that house that each servant should invest something of his own in each of the merchant's ventures. Whittington had nothing but his cat, and reluctantly sent it off on a voyage to Barbary. Shortly after, he became discontented with his lot and ran away, but got only as far as the foot of Highgate Hill, where he sat down to rest. It was here that he heard Bow Bells ring a message he translated as, "Turn again, Dick Whittington, thrice lord mayor of London town." On the strength of this promise he returned to his work and was soon rewarded by the news that his cat had rid the Moorish King of a plague of mice, and had been sold for a treasure richer than all his master's cargo.

Perhaps this is true. It is certainly true that Richard Whittington was three times mayor of London in the time of Henry V, whose war in France he financed out of his own pocket. His first term was about the time Chaucer was writing *The Canterbury Tales,* Jack Straw was leading his rebellion, and Prince Hal and Falstaff were holding up pilgrims on Gadshill, including, we hope, the Wife of Bath and Chaucer himself.

We believe there is only one walk in all of London that is the equal of the one you have just taken.
To take it, start where you now stand, and retrace your steps.

—DANIEL CURLEY, ROGER EBERT AND JACK LANE

Index of Places